AMAZING BIRD FACTS

Anita Ganeri
Illustrated by Jack McCarthy
and Kate Osborne
Consultant: Sylvia Sullivan
Editor: Anne Civardi
Designed by Katrina ffiske

Contents

MALLARD PRESS

An imprint of BDD Promotional Book Company, Inc., 666 Fifth Avenue, New York, N.Y. 10103

All About Birds

The first bird lived on the Earth about 150 million years ago. It was about the size of a pigeon and was called archaeopteryx. Scientists think that it was probably descended from a type of small, two-legged dinosaur.

Today there are about 8,600 different species of birds in the world. They range in size from the smallest hummingbirds, which are no bigger than large moths, to the huge ostrich which is taller than a very tall man.

Lightweight Fliers

To fly well, a bird needs to be as light as possible. Most birds have hollow bones to save weight. A big bird, such as the golden eagle, which may have a wingspan of over 7.5 ft (2.3 m), weighs about the same as a newborn baby.

Birds have more bones in their necks than most other animals. Most mammals, even giraffes, have seven neck bones. Herons have up to 17 bones in their long necks so that they can catch their food and clean their feathers.

A small bird's heart may beat at over 600 beats a minute.

Feathers make up about $\frac{1}{6}$ of a bird's weight. Many birds have feathers which blend in with their backgrounds and help them hide from their enemies.

Some birds swallow stones which help grind up their food.

A large breastbone supports the bird's strong flight muscles.

Most birds have three or four toes. Some use them to grip onto branches, others have webbed feet for swimming and some have big, sharp talons to catch their prey.

Bird Brain

Birds have small brains compared with human beings and are not good at learning to do things. But they are born with a huge store of built-in knowledge.

This is called instinct and tells them how to behave automatically. They also copy what their parents do. Crows are probably the brainiest birds.

Sleeping Tight

Many birds sleep perched high up on the branches of trees. As they land, their toes automatically grip the branch and stay locked in place so that the birds do not fall off when they go to sleep. Turtle doves fluff up their feathers and put their heads under a wing for the night.

Birds have the highest body temperature of all warm-blooded animals.

Birds have very strong, light beaks which constantly grow and wear down during their lifetime. They do not have any teeth.

Bird Lives

Many wild birds are killed before they die of old age. Few small birds survive the first year of life. They are hunted by cats and other animals, hit by cars or die of diseases. The oldest known wild bird is a royal albatross, called "Grandma". She is about 62 years old.

Under Threat

A thousand species of birds are in danger of dying out as their homes are being destroyed. Dusky seaside sparrows used to live in the salt marshes of Florida. They died when the marshes were drained to make land for building.

Did You Know?

Most birds have feathers covering most of their bodies, apart from their beaks and feet. They usually shed their battered and worn out feathers and grow new ones once a year. They do not shed them all at once so that they are still able to fly. This is called molting.

A bird's leg looks as if it is bending the wrong way, with the knee pointing backwards instead of forwards. But this joint is actually the bird's ankle, not its knee at all. Its knee joint is higher up its leg, hidden by lots of feathers. Some big birds have a powerful kick.

Over half the birds in the world are songbirds. They use their voices to attract a mate, to "talk" to other birds in the flock or to warn off any intruders from their territory. Most birds sing at dawn or dusk when the air is still and their song carries further.

3

Fantastic Feathers

Birds are the only animals in the world that have feathers. These are made of a special material, called keratin, which is strong and flexible. Keratin also makes our nails and hair, reptiles' scales and rhinos' horns.

In the Pink

If flamingos do not have the right food, their feathers fade from pink to a dull gray. In the wild, they eat shrimps and tiny water plants, called algae, which contain a special color called carotene.

Camouflage Colors

Asian hanging parrots sleep and feed hanging upside down on the branches of dead trees. They look just like big bunches of leaves and are left alone by enemies.

Ptarmigans live in the Arctic and on cold mountains. They change color with the seasons and are difficult to spot. In the Summer, their feathers are a speckled brown, like plants and rocks. In the Winter, they turn white to match the ice and snow.

Ant Bath

Most birds bathe in dust and water to clean fleas and lice off their feathers. A jay uses the acid made by ants. It stands on an ants' nest and lets hundreds of ants crawl all over its body.

Powder and Comb

Herons have some feathers which crumble into powder. They rub this powder into the other feathers to clean off slime after they have been catching eels. The powder and slime collects into large lumps which a heron combs out with a special claw on its third toe.

Dazzling Eyes

To attract a mate, a peacock fans out his wonderful tail feathers and shakes them. Each one of the 200 feathers is decorated with a "glittering" eye. Scientists think that a female is hypnotized by this dazzling display.

Did You Know?

Birds have different types of feathers for different jobs. Soft, fluffy down feathers keep them warm. The feathers covering their bodies and giving them shape, are called "contour" feathers. They use tail feathers for steering in the air and for display, and long, stiff wing feathers for flying.

Feathers are made of a shaft in the middle with about 100 hook-like barbs on each side. The barbs fit together like the teeth of a zipper. If the feathers get out of shape, a bird grooms them with its beak.

Many male birds have more colorful feathers than females. A female peacock, called a peahen, has dull brown feathers.

A swan has more feathers than any other bird – over 25,000. About 20,000 feathers are on its head and neck. The tiny ruby-throated hummingbird has only 940 feathers.

A Japanese phoenix fowl has the longest feathers. Its tail feathers can be up to 35 ft (10.6 m) long – longer than three cars in a line.

In zoos and bird sanctuaries, flamingos are fed carrot juice to keep their feathers "in the pink".

Champions of the Air

Birds are the champion fliers of the animal world. They are perfectly designed for life in the air. Their strong wings are slightly curved to keep them airborne and their light bodies are streamlined for speed through the air.

Birds can fly faster and further than any other animal, including bats and insects. They can cruise along for days without landing, turn quickly in mid-air, dive down at high speed or soar for hours on rising currents of warm air.

High Flier

Rüppell's griffon vultures usually fly as high as 5,000 ft (1,500 m). In 1973, one of them crashed into an aircraft flying at 37,000 ft (11,270 m). That is about 8,200 ft (2,500 m) higher than Mount Everest, the tallest mountain in the world.

Fast Flappers

Hummingbirds can fly forwards, backwards, sideways, and up and down. They can hover in front of a flower to feed on the nectar deep inside. To stay quite still, they beat their wings up to 90 times a second, faster than any other bird.

Express Bird

The peregrine falcon is the fastest flier in the world. It dives down on its prey at 112 mph (180 km/h) – as fast as an express train. As it dives, or stoops, it folds back its wings and hits its prey with its sharp talons, often killing it with one powerful blow.

Crash Landing

Tinamous, which live in South America, are one of the world's worst fliers. They dash off at such speed that they soon become too tired to fly at all.

Sometimes they crash into trees, badly wounding or even killing themselves. They may make an emergency landing in the middle of a lake or river. Fortunately, they are good swimmers.

Graceful Glider

The slim, pointed wings of the wandering albatross are the longest in the world. They may measure up to 12 ft (3.7 m) from wing tip to wing tip.

This albatross glides over the Southern Ocean, using warm air currents to keep aloft. It can fly 560 miles (900 km) in a day, hardly ever flapping its wings.

Nesting on the tops and hillsides of islands, it uses the wind to help it to take off.

Did You Know?

Huge Andean condors have the biggest wings in the world. They can soar for hours, like a glider, as they search for food on high mountains. They do not need to flap their wings as they are pushed upwards by rising currents of warm air.

About half of all the birds in the world can reach speeds of over 40 mph (64 km/h).

A wandering albatross may fly nearly 205,000 miles (330,000 km) in a year, enough to go eight times around the world.

When a common swift leaves its nest, it spends the next two or three years in the air. It eats, drinks, mates and sleeps on the wing. When it finally lands, it may have flown for 45,000 miles (72,000 km) without stopping.

Birds' wings vary according to how they live and what they eat. Geese have long, broad wings for extra lift when taking off from water. Swifts have long, pointed wings so they can turn quickly to catch flying insects. Gulls have long, slim wings for gliding.

The heaviest flying birds are great bustards. They weigh about as much as 12 chickens.

Somewhere to Live

Birds live in all parts of the world. Flocks of parrots fly through hot, steamy jungles. Penguins survive in the freezing Antarctic. Birds of prey soar over high mountain peaks and huge albatrosses glide over the oceans.

Birds are able to live in so many different places because they are warm-blooded. Their body temperatures stay the same, no matter how hot or cold the weather is. Some have very clever ways of surviving.

Rainforest Residents

Hundreds of different kinds of birds live in the rain forests of South America. The trees and plants grow very fast and there is plenty of fruit and insects for the birds to eat.

Desert Dwellers

The roadrunner lives in the deserts of North America. It can run at speeds of up to 25 mph (40 km/h). To catch snakes to eat, it chases around them until they are too tired to strike. Then it stabs them with its sharp beak.

A sand grouse may fly up to 25 miles (40 km) to get water for its chicks. At a waterhole, it soaks its breast feathers with water. Then it flies back to the chicks who suck the water off their mother's feathers.

Elf owls shelter from the burning daytime heat in holes in giant saguaro cacti. The cacti's sharp spines keep away any enemies. At night, the owls leave the holes, which may be empty woodpecker nests, to hunt for food.

Parrots and macaws live in noisy flocks in the forests. They use their hooked beaks for cracking open seeds and nuts, and also as an extra foot for climbing trees.

Many of these tropical birds have brightly colored feathers. They live high up in the treetops where there is lots of bright sunlight. Dull colored birds live on the ground where it is dark and gloomy.

Burrow Borrowers

Burrowing owls live in the deserts of North America. These tiny, long-legged owls often live in the empty burrows of prairie dogs, badgers, ground squirrels and skunks. To make the holes bigger, they scrape away the earth with their powerful clawed feet.

Did You Know?

There are no penguins at the Arctic. Most penguins live in the the Antarctic. They have thick, waterproof feathers and a layer of blubber, or fat, under their skins to keep them warm. The feathers and down also trap air which helps to insulate the birds.

Three house sparrows made their home 2,100 ft (640 m) down a coal mine in Yorkshire, England. They lived there for three years.

White storks often build their stick nests on top of chimney stacks, telephone poles and roofs.

Spine Chilling

There are 14 species of Darwin's finches on the Galapagos Islands. Each type has a different beak for eating a different kind of food. Seed eaters have short, thick bills, insect eaters have long, straight beaks, and those that sip nectar have long, curved beaks.

A woodpecker finch uses a cactus spine to poke into holes and pick out insects and grubs.

A toucan's colorful beak looks heavy but it is hollow and very light. Toucans use their beaks to reach fruit among the leaves. They toss the fruit up into the air and catch it in their throats.

Feathered Friends

All birds need to find a mate so that they can breed and have babies. Some only have one partner throughout their lives, others have many. Competition for females can be very fierce and male birds have special ways of attracting them.

Many, such as peacocks and birds of paradise, show off their brilliantly-colored feathers to impress a mate. Others sing, dance or display their skills as builders or hunters. Japanese cranes sing together and point their bills skywards when they court.

In Paradise

A male Count Raggi's bird of paradise has long red plumes on his back. He swings upside-down on a branch, fanning out his handsome plumes to dazzle female birds. A female chooses the bird with the most beautiful feathers and the best display as her mate.

Love in the Air

Male sea eagles impress females with their incredible flying skills. The male flies high up into the sky and then dives down towards the female. She turns upside-down, they grip each other's claws and cartwheel together through the air.

Come into My Bower

Bowerbirds work hard to find a mate. The male satin bowerbird builds two neat rows of twigs. He decorates his "bower" with blue feathers, flowers and even bits of colorful plastic.

Then he paints the twigs with blue berry juice. When he has finished, a female bowerbird comes to inspect his leafy shelter. If she likes it, she will stay and mate with the male.

As many as ten Count Raggi's males may display in the same tree. But usually the females choose only one bird to mate with and the other males do not mate at all.

Did You Know?

Many birds sing songs to attract a mate. One of the loudest is made by a male bellbird. It sounds like a large, clanging bell and can be heard over 0.6 miles (1 km) away. When a female comes close, the male leaps and dances, then calls again.

Puffins grow bright blue, red and yellow beaks to attract a mate in the breeding season. In late Summer, the outer layer of beak falls off, leaving them with smaller, gray beaks for Winter. Puffins are the only birds that shed, or molt, their beaks.

Male and female Adélie penguins look so alike that it is difficult for them to tell each other apart. But a male has a special way of finding a mate. He drops a pebble at the feet of a possible "wife". If the penguin bows, she is female and they mate. If the penguin pecks him hard, then he is a male!

When birds are kept in captivity, they sometimes get confused about mates. A gander once fell in love with a garbage can. He showed no interest when he was introduced to a female goose!

Ballooning Love

Male frigatebirds have big, red pouches under their chins. They blow them up like balloons to attract females. A male may keep his pouch inflated for hours before a female chooses him. She rubs her head against his chest to show her interest.

Dancing Partners

Great crested grebes perform a strange dance before they mate. They shake their heads and then dive under the water. When they come up again, they race across the water side by side. At the end of the dance, they give each other gifts of waterweed.

Busy Builders

Birds need a safe place to lay their eggs and rear their young. Most build strong, warm nests which come in many different shapes and sizes. As well as making them in trees and bushes, they build them in some very unusual places.

They nest on the tops of tall chimneys, in river banks, in hollow trees and garden sheds, and even in mailboxes and watering cans. Many birds use twigs and grass, but some use much stranger materials for their nests.

Nut-sized Nests

Hummingbirds build the smallest nests. A vervain hummingbird's nest is only as big as half a walnut. A bee hummingbird's nest is even smaller, about the size of a hazelnut. Hummingbirds are too small to build with twigs. Instead they use silk from cobwebs to make their tiny nests.

High and Mighty

The biggest nests of sticks and twigs are built by bald eagles. Every year, they come back to the same nest and add more branches. The birds get new material by bouncing on tree branches until they snap off.

All Sealed In

Hornbills build their nests inside hollow tree trunks. To keep the eggs safe from hungry monkeys and snakes, the female is sealed in. The male blocks the nest entrance with mud and birds' droppings, leaving a small slit to pass food through to her.

Leafy Nests

To make its amazing nest, the clever tailorbird sews leaves together. He uses his beak as a needle to make holes in the leaves, and strands of cobweb as thread. He even ties a knot at the end of the thread.

The village weaver builds his nest out of grass and leaves. Using his beak and feet, he knots a blade of grass to a branch to form a ring. Then he weaves grass and leaf strips into this frame to make a round nest.

Some of these nests are more than 50 years old. They can be over 18 ft (6 m) high, 9 ft (3 m) across and weigh as much as two small cars. Sometimes they get so heavy that they crash to the ground.

Did You Know?

Penduline tits make such warm, fluffy nests that some children in eastern Europe collect them and use them as slippers.

Kingfishers lay their eggs in tunnels in the river bank.

A bay-winged cowbird does not make a nest of its own. It steals one from another bird.

A linnet was once found nesting on the top of a cauliflower. It had laid four eggs!

Honeyguides, in Australia, line their nests with hair for warmth. They pluck the hair from horses' manes and from peoples' heads!

Some birds use strange and very uncomfortable things to make their nests. One crow built its nest completely out of barbed wire. Another, in India, was made of gold spectacle frames.

Some swiflets make their nests out of nothing but their own saliva. These nests are often stolen and made into bird's-nest soup which is served in many Chinese restaurants.

Mounds of Earth

The mallee fowl builds the biggest nest of all – a huge mound of earth and plants covered with sand. It may be up to 15 ft (4.6 m) high and over 35 ft (10.6 m) across.

The female lays her eggs inside the enormous mound. The heat from the rotting plants keeps the eggs warm until they hatch about eight months later.

13

Eggs and Baby Birds

All birds lay eggs which hatch into baby birds. Some lay just one egg, others can lay four times their own weight in eggs. Birds' eggs come in different sizes and colors. The kind of eggs a bird lays depends on how and where it lives.

Birds' eggs need to be kept warm, but not overheated, until they hatch so that the chicks inside do not die. Many of the chicks are fed by their parents while they learn how to fly and how to find food for themselves.

Super Eggs

Ostriches lay the largest eggs of all birds. They weigh about 3 lbs (1.3 kg), over 4,000 times more than the smallest bird's eggs, laid by the vervain hummingbird. The eggs are strong enough to support the weight of two large people!

Hatching Out

When it is ready to hatch, a chick breaks its eggshell with a bony knob on the end of its beak. This is called its "egg tooth". The tooth soon drops off. Hatching usually takes about an hour but albatross chicks may take a week to break out of their tough shells.

Ready for Take-off

Baby storks stand on the edge of their nest and flap their wings to practice flying. Gannet chicks practice too. They are born on steep sea cliffs and stand facing the cliff so that they do not accidentally fly off too soon.

Hungry Chicks

Many parent birds, like this golden oriole, work very hard bringing food for their hungry chicks. Great tits may have as many as 10 babies to feed. They may make over 700 trips to their nests with food each day.

The story of ostriches burying their heads in the sand comes from the way females sit on their eggs. They lay their necks, covered with brown feathers, on the ground to make them look like piles of earth. This is to fool their enemies so that they leave the nests alone.

A female ostrich may lay as many as 10 eggs at a time. Sometimes two or three ostriches lay their eggs together in the same place.

Cooling Down

Birds that live in very hot places have to make sure that their eggs do not overheat. The blacksmith plover from East Africa stretches her wings over her eggs to shade them from the heat of the Sun.

Keeping Warm

Eggs need to be kept at a temperature of about 95°F (35°C) so that they hatch properly. The female bird usually sits on the eggs to keep them warm.

The great spotted woodpecker sits on hers for about 10 days. The wandering albatross sits on her eggs for 2½ months before they hatch.

Did You Know?

The largest eggs of all were laid by the elephant bird from Madagascar. This bird is now extinct but it looked like a giant emu. Its eggs were bigger than dinosaur eggs and as big as 180 hens' eggs.

When emu eggs are laid, they are dark green. After a few days they turn a glossy black.

Flamingo chicks are fed on a milky liquid from their parents' mouths. The "milk" is bright red.

The European cuckoo lays its eggs in other birds' nests. It leaves the foster-mother to look after the chick, which may grow much bigger than her. The cuckoo's eggs usually have similar markings and coloring to the "host's" eggs.

Finding Food

Flying, breeding and looking after its chicks uses up a huge amount of a bird's energy. Like people, birds get energy from the food they eat. Most of them need regular meals and they spend a lot of time looking for the right food.

Birds' bills often have special features to help them catch a particular type of food. They do not have teeth and so they cannot chew their food. Instead, they grind it up in a special part of their stomachs, called a gizzard.

Full Pouches

Pelicans have huge, stretchy pouches of skin under their bills. They use these like nets to scoop fish out of the water to eat.

When a pelican catches the fish in its pouch, it also takes in a lot of seawater. As the bird lifts its head from the water, its huge bill points downwards, allowing water to drain out. Then, with a toss of its head, it swallows the fish whole.

Greedy Vultures

Griffon vultures in Africa eat the remains of animals killed by lions or cheetahs. When they see a carcass, they flock to the dead animal. They can strip an antelope to the bone in just 20 minutes. Vultures have bare heads and necks so their feathers do not get clogged with blood.

Brown pelicans are expert divers and plunge into the water to catch fish that live deeper down.

Snipe Snouts

Common snipes usually live near water. Outside the breeding season, they are often found in big flocks by the seaside. Snipes have long, sensitive beaks which they use to probe deep into wet mud or sand in search of worms. They can open their beaks under the ground to catch the worms.

Thief in the Sky

Arctic skuas do not catch their own food. They steal it from other birds. They chase terns and puffins in the air and force them to drop their catch of fish. Then they gobble down their easy meals.

Gulls often hover close to pelicans and try to steal some of their fish.

Sticky Tongues

Woodpeckers chisel holes in tree trunks with their strong, pointed beaks. Then they use their long, sticky, or barbed, tongues to search inside the holes for grubs and insects to eat. Their tongues can stretch 4 in (10 cm) out of their beaks.

Did You Know?

Flamingos use their curved beaks like sieves to strain food out of the water. They hold their beaks upside-down and suck water in. Then they push the water out with their tongues, leaving behind tiny plants and shrimps which they eat.

Seagulls drop shellfish from high in the air to smash them open on the rocks below.

Wrybills in New Zealand are the only birds whose beaks curve to one side.

The sides of a merganser duck's beak are serrated, like a saw, to trap fish.

A sword-billed hummingbird's beak is four times the length of its body. It uses it to sip nectar from deep inside flowers.

Crossbills are the only birds that can reach the seeds inside pine cones because they have special, crossed-over bills. Baby crossbills are born with straight beaks but they soon cross over.

17

Hunters of the Skies

Birds of prey are the greatest hunters of the bird world. They swoop and soar in the air, looking for something to eat with their superb eyes. Using their powerful wings, they dive down to catch their prey.

These cruel-looking birds eat meat of all kinds including rabbits, birds, snakes, insects and fish. They hold their prey with their sharp talons and tear it apart with their hooked beaks.

Monkey Hunter

The huge harpy eagles, which live in the rain forests of South America, are one of the most powerful eagles. They fly at top speed through the trees, dodging the branches, and snatch monkeys, sloths, birds and even porcupines to eat.

Secretary Bird

A secretary bird looks more like a stork than a hawk. It is the only bird of prey that hunts on foot, striding through the grass. It feeds mainly on snakes which it quickly kicks to death with its long, powerful legs.

Honey for Tea

A honey buzzard watches for bees and follows them back to their nest. Then it digs up the nest to get at the grubs and honey inside. The bees try to sting the buzzard but the thick feathers on its head protect it.

Bone Breakers

Lammergeiers are huge vultures. They are nicknamed "bone breakers" because of the way they get their food. They carry bones of dead animals high into the air and drop them onto rocks below, smashing them open. Then they eat the marrow inside.

These fierce birds build large messy nests, usually high up in the fork of a giant silk-cotton tree.

Did You Know?

Birds of prey have the best eyesight of any animal. A hawk has bigger eyes than a human being and can see about eight times better over long distances.

Most birds of prey eat meat but the palm nut vulture is a vegetarian. It mainly eats fruit from the oil palm tree, though it will also eat fish and shellfish.

A huge white-tailed eagle once snatched a four-year-old girl from a farm in Norway. It set off for its nest on a mountainside but dropped her on a rocky ledge. She was soon rescued.

An Andean condor is the biggest bird of prey. It weighs over 300 times more than the smallest bird of prey, a tiny Philippine falconet.

In the Andes, Indians sometimes eat condors' eyes because they believe this will improve their own eyesight.

The Everglade kite only eats one type of water snail. It grabs the snails with its feet and pulls them out with its beak which fits exactly inside the shells.

Harpy eagles hatch out a single egg every other year. The parents feed the chick until it is at least nine months old and able to fly well.

Fishing with Feet

Ospreys fly low over the water and catch fish with their feet. They have long, sharp claws and spikes on their toes for getting a good grip on the slippery fish. They grip so tightly that they are sometimes dragged under the water by very large fish.

19

On the Water

Many different types of birds live near fresh water, on the banks of rivers, lakes and ponds. Their bodies are perfectly suited to their lives spent in the water, mud and reeds.

Many water birds have webbed feet for swimming. They also have waterproof feathers so that they do not get wet. And they have some very special and unusual ways of catching their food.

Fishing Bait

Green herons use bait to catch fish, just like fishermen. The heron stands at the water's edge and drops in a tempting insect. It stands absolutely still and waits for a fish to take the bait. Then it strikes and spears the fish with its beak.

Lily Trotters

Jacanas have the longest toes of any bird. They open out their toes to spread their weight as they walk or sprint across lily leaves and other floating plants.

Snake Neck

The anhinga is also called the snake bird. This is because its long neck looks like a slithering snake as it swims across the water. This strange-looking bird skewers fish with its sharp beak, tosses them into the air and swallows them in one gulp.

As soon as jacana chicks are able to use their long-toed feet well enough, their parents lead them across the water to hunt for food.

Swirling Torrents

Torrent ducks live on fast-flowing rivers in South America. They are not swept away by the strong currents because they are very strong swimmers. They also have claws on their feet for gripping the slippery rocks.

Reed Nester

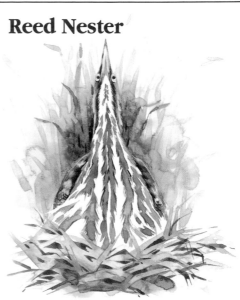

Bitterns live in reed beds on the edges of lakes and ponds. They use the reeds to build their nests which hang over the water. To hide from its enemies, a bittern stands very straight and still. It matches the reeds so closely that it is almost impossible to spot.

Jacanas feed mostly on insects, snails, fish and the seeds of water plants which they find in ponds, lagoons and marshes.

Did You Know?

Phalaropes swim around and around in circles, stirring the water into whirlpools. Fish and other small creatures are sucked into the center of the whirlpools where they are easy to catch.

Grebes are said to swallow stones to make themselves heavier so they can dive deeper.

Black herons shade the water with their outstretched wings so they can see the fish more easily.

Trumpeter swans are too heavy to take off from a standing start. To build up enough speed to get into the air, they flap their big wings and run across the water, like an aircraft on a runway.

Dippers dive underwater to find insects, worms and small fish to eat. They walk along river and stream beds, flicking their wings to keep their balance. Dippers have such thick, warm feathers that they can feed under the ice.

Many water birds oil their feathers to make them waterproof.

Life on the Waves

There are about 300 types of sea birds. Some soar over the open oceans, some dive from steep cliffs to catch fish to eat. Others live along the seashore, searching the sand and mud for food.

At breeding time, the sea coast and cliffs are thronged with birds. Sea birds lay their eggs on the cliff ledges, in burrows on the cliff tops and even on sandy or stony beaches.

Fantastic Frigates

Frigatebirds cannot swim but they can fly faster than any other sea bird. With its long wings and forked tail, the magnificent frigatebird can reach speeds of over 93 mph (150 km/h) in the air.

They often steal their food from other birds in mid-air. Sometimes they catch their own food, snatching flying fish from above the waves or taking squid and jellyfish from the top of the water.

Champion Penguins

Gentoo penguins are the fastest of all swimming birds. In short bursts, they can reach a top speed of more than 16.5 mph (27 km/h). This is about three times faster than the fastest person can swim.

Did You Know?

Sea birds sometimes look as if they have runny noses. This is how they get rid of all the harmful salt they take in from sea water as they feed. Special glands in their heads take the salt out of the water. It then trickles out of the birds' noses.

The ringed plover lays its eggs on a pebbly beach. If an intruder comes too close, the plover runs off, trailing one wing along as if it is broken to fool the enemy. At a safe distance from the nest, she suddenly recovers and flies back to look after her eggs.

Guillemots lay their eggs on bare, narrow, crowded cliff ledges. The eggs are a special pear-shape so that they do not roll off.

The wandering albatross lays the biggest eggs of any sea bird. One weighs as much as nine hen's eggs.

Frigatebird chicks have to be protected all the time as their nests are often torn apart by other frigatebirds looking for nesting materials. Sometimes they also eat the chicks.

The chicks stay in the nest for about five months. Even after learning to fly, they return to the nest to be fed until they are over a year old.

Dive Bombers

To catch fish, gannets dive into the sea from heights of as much as 148 ft (45 m). The soft bone around their heads and air sacs around their throats and breasts cushion their bodies as they hit the hard water.

Water Walker

The Wilson's storm petrel has big parasol wings that allow it to fly very slowly without stalling. About the size of a thrush, it looks as if it is skipping over the sea. Sometimes it flies so low, searching for food, that its feet patter on the surface.

Oyster Hammer

Oystercatchers feed along the seashore. They use their strong, blunt beaks as hammers to chip through the hard shell of a crab, mussel or cockle. Often the birds will wash the mussel or cockle before swallowing it.

Spitting Fulmars

Fulmars spit at their enemies to drive them away from their nests. The spit is a type of oil made inside the fulmar's stomach from the food that it eats. It has a terrible smell!

Night Birds

Only a few birds come out at night. Called nocturnal birds, most of them are owls. These night hunters have all sorts of advantages over birds that are active during the day. In the dark, they have less competition for food and they are much safer from their enemies. They also have some clever ways of finding their way in the dark, and of finding their food.

All Eyes and Ears

An owl has huge eyes for seeing in the dark. It cannot swivel its eyes to look to the side but can turn its whole head around. It can also look backwards and upside-down. Some owls can see 50 times better in the dark than a human being.

Owls have excellent hearing to listen out for their prey of mice, small animals and birds. Their ears are long slits hidden near their eyes. Some owls have one ear bigger than the other for judging exactly where a sound is coming from.

Home for the Night

Manx shearwaters hunt for fish during the day. At night they come ashore to their burrows on the cliff tops. They live in huge colonies, sometimes of over 100,000 birds. Returning home only at night keeps the birds safe from attacks by gulls.

Smelling at Night

Kiwis hunt at night for worms and insects to eat. They are unusual birds because they use their noses to smell for food. Most birds have nostrils at the base of their beak but a kiwi has its at the tip of its long beak.

Bat hawks feed at dusk because their prey only comes out in the evening. The hawks catch the bats as they leave their roosts in caves or trees to feed.

The rare kakapo in New Zealand is the only parrot that cannot fly. It feeds at night on grass, ferns and berries. The male birds have loud booming cries to attract the females in the dark.

The curious kagu bird in New Caledonia spends most of its time on the ground. It hunts for food at night, running quickly and then standing still as it looks for worms, grubs and insects to eat.

Swallow-tailed gulls live on the Galapagos Islands. They are the only nocturnal gulls known. They eat squid and fish, spotting them in the dark with their large eyes.

Owls take their prey completely by surprise because they can fly without making any noise. They swoop down on a mouse and grab it with their sharp claws, often swallowing it whole. Later, they vomit up a pellet of fur, feathers, beaks or bones.

Good Night Hunters

Nightjars are such good night hunters that they can dive down and catch moths, mosquitoes and other insects in mid-air. They can open their small beaks very wide. Bristles on the sides of their mouths may help them to feel for food in the dark.

Oilbird Echoes

Oilbirds live deep inside dark caves. They find their way, as bats do, by using echo-location.

The birds make lots of clicking sounds which hit obstacles and send back echoes. The echoes tell them how far they are from other birds and the cave walls.

Flocking Together

Many birds spend much of their lives on their own, only looking for company when they are ready to mate. Others gather at night in trees or caves when they roost or sleep.

Some birds are very sociable. They live and travel in large flocks, helping each other to find food and look after their young. Birds also form special relationships with other animals and sometimes with people.

Sociable Birds

Social weavers, which are about the size of a sparrow, live together in big groups in Africa. They build huge nests that look like straw roofs high up in the treetops. Below the roofs, hundreds of birds build their own separate nests.

Easy Meals

Carmine bee-eaters in Africa hitch lifts on the backs of kori bustards. As a bustard runs along, it disturbs flies and other insects which swarm out of the way of its feet. The bee-eaters quickly snap up the insects.

Team Work

White pelicans work in teams to catch fish. Large groups fly in a horseshoe shape, flapping their wings and beating their feet to drive the fish into the middle. Then they plunge their bills into the water to catch them.

Ant Eggs

Rufous woodpeckers in Asia have a special relationship with stinging tree ants. They lay their eggs in the ants' round nests, which are about the size of a soccer ball. The eggs are protected by the ants which sting any intruders.

Sometimes other birds, such as finches and falcons, take over empty weavers' nests and make a snug home for themselves.

The birds enter the nests through a tunnel of stiff straw. These tunnels make it hard for any predator to get inside and eat the eggs.

Did You Know?

Jackdaws choose a mate when they are only a year old. They stay together for the rest of their lives, as long as 64 years.

Parrots, budgerigars and mynah birds can copy the way people speak. The most talkative caged bird was an African gray parrot called Prudle. She could say about 800 words.

The last passenger pigeon in the world died in a zoo in 1914. Just 100 years before, these pigeons flew over the US in flocks of over 2 million strong, the biggest flocks ever seen.

An amazing 32 million red-billed queleas were found in one roost in the Sudan in Africa.

Some geese and ducks leave their chicks in "nurseries". Groups of over a hundred eider ducks are looked after by an "aunty" while their mothers search for food.

Keeping in Touch

Birds use songs and calls to keep in touch with each other and to warn away intruders. Crows have quite a complicated language with about 300 sounds. Like people, crows in different parts of the world speak different languages.

Traveling Birds

Every Winter, many birds leave their breeding grounds and fly long distances to warmer places where it is easier to find plenty of food. The following Spring, they return to their homes to breed. This traveling is called migration.

Many birds find their way back to the same nesting place year after year. Scientists are still not sure how they navigate so accurately. They may use the Sun and stars as guides, or certain landmarks, such as rivers, valleys and mountains.

On the March

In the Antarctic, Adélie penguins spend the Winter far out at sea, feeding on small fish and krill. In September and October, millions of birds return to their breeding grounds on the snow and ice.

As they cannot fly, the penguins sometimes have to waddle up to 200 miles (320 km) across the sea ice. Even when the ground is covered with snow, they find their way back to their old nesting sites.

Straight Ahead

Each Winter, bristle-thighed curlews fly about 5,600 miles (9,000 km) from Alaska to tiny islands in the Pacific Ocean. They always follow the same, straight route south. Even if the wind blows them off course, they quickly find their way again.

Long-distance Traveler

The Arctic tern is the greatest traveler of all. Each year, it flies from the Arctic to the Antarctic and back again. This is a round trip of about 25,600 miles (40,000 km). In its lifetime a tern flies the same distance as to the Moon and back.

The penguins seem to use the Sun to guide them. On cloudy days, they lose their way but head in the right direction again when the Sun comes out.

Did You Know?

One of the fastest travelers is an American golden plover. It flies non-stop from the Aleutian Islands to Hawaii, about 2,050 miles (3,300 km) away. It does this in just $1^{1}/_{2}$ days, beating its wings over 250,000 times.

Every Fall, thousands of tiny ruby-throated hummingbirds fly over 1,800 miles (3,000 km) across the USA to spend the Winter in Central America. On the way, they fly over 500 miles (800 km) of water.

Long ago, people did not know where birds went in the Winter. Some thought that they flew to the Moon or sheltered from the cold at the bottom of ponds!

Down the Mountain

Mountain quails in North America make one of the shortest trips. In the Fall, they leave their high mountain nests and walk in single file down to the valley. They only travel about 4,600 ft (1,400 m).

Over the Top

On their migration, huge flocks of bar-headed geese have to cross over the Himalayas, the highest mountains in the world. They fly at heights of up to 5 miles (8 km). This is almost as high as a jet aircraft. Most migrating birds fly below 300 ft (91 m).

Did You Know?

Long-legged Runner

An ostrich has small wings and is much too heavy to fly but it can run very fast. At top speed it can race along at over 43 mph (70 km/h), faster than a racehorse.

Smallest of All

The world's smallest bird is the bee hummingbird which lives in Cuba. It is only the size of an ostrich's eye. Fully-grown males are just 2.2 in (5.7 cm) long. They weigh less than a sugar cube.

Deep Divers

Emperor penguins can dive deeper than any other bird. Ten penguins in Antarctica dived down to 870 ft (265 m). One penguin stayed under the water for 18 minutes. The deepest dive by a person holding his breath is 344 ft (105 m).

Big Sleeper

The poorwill of North America hibernates in the Winter. It builds up as much fat in its body as it can and then settles down to sleep in a hole for several months, living off the fat until the following Spring.

Fussy Cleaners

Lyrebirds live in gullies in the forests of Australia and are rarely seen. The female lyrebird is very fussy about her nest. She picks up all the droppings and puts them in a stream or river.

Pecking Order

A flock of chickens has a strict social order. This means that the top bird eats first, followed by the next one, and so on down the line. The top bird keeps its position by pecking any birds which do not obey the order. The second bird may peck any bird except the top bird, and so on.

Anything to Eat?

Ostriches swallow pebbles or stones to help them grind up their food. Sometimes they swallow much stranger things. An ostrich which died in London Zoo, England, had an amazing assortment of objects in its stomach. They included coins, gloves, rope, a pencil and a camera film.

Heavy Head

The helmeted hornbill has a very heavy skull. Its head makes up $\frac{1}{10}$ of its total body weight. Luckily, the hornbill also has a very long tail, almost 3 ft (1 m) long. This stops it from overbalancing and toppling onto its head!

The Biggest Bird

The North African ostrich is the biggest bird in the world. Male ostriches can be up to 9 ft (2.7 m) tall and weigh as much as two heavy people.

What a Coup!

There are thought to be about 100 billion birds in the world. Of these, over 8 billion are chickens. This is enough for every person in the world to have $1\frac{1}{2}$ chickens each.

Rare Bird

Ivory-billed woodpeckers are one of the rarest birds in the world and may now be extinct in the southern parts of the US. They live in swampy forests. Indian chiefs used to decorate their belts with the woodpeckers' beaks and claws.

Bird Droppings

Cormorants' guano, or droppings, make a very rich fertilizer. More than 5 million cormorants used to live along the coasts of Peru. In places, their droppings were 164 ft (50 m) deep.

Good Enough to Eat

The great auk, a flightless seabird, looked like a penguin. The last one was killed in 1844. People ate the auks' meat and eggs, and used their fat for oil lamps. They were also afraid of them and even burnt them as witches!

Earth Eaters

Scarlet macaws usually live in pairs, but several times a year they gather in huge flocks and fly to special sites on the river bank to eat the soil. The plant seeds which they normally eat can be poisonous. The soil contains minerals which stops the poison from having any bad effects on the birds.

Claws for Climbing

Hoatzin chicks are born in nests above the water in mangrove swamps. If they are frightened, they jump into the water. To get back to their nests, the chicks have small claws on their wrists which they use for climbing up the trees.

Old Birds

The oldest known bird in captivity was a cockatoo, called Cocky. When he died he was thought to be at least 80 years old, and maybe even 82.

Fast Flippers

Penguins cannot fly through the air but they "fly" underwater. Using their wings as flippers, they reach speeds of 25 mph (40 km/h). On land, penguins look clumsy because they cannot fold their wings.

Dead as a Dodo

Some of the most famous extinct birds could not fly. The dodo was discovered in Mauritius by European settlers in 1599. The settlers killed so many dodos for their meat and eggs that, just 100 years later, there were no dodos left.

Captive Condors

There are no Californian condors left in the wild. But zoos are trying to breed them and return them to their natural homes. The first condor chick born in captivity hatched out in the San Diego Zoo. Its keepers fed it using a leather condor-head puppet so that it would learn to behave normally and could survive in the wild.

Horny Helmets

Cassowaries live in the rain forests of Australia and Papua New Guinea. They crash through the thick undergrowth, using the horny helmets on their heads as battering rams. A cassowary defends itself by kicking its enemies. One good kick could kill a person.

Index

First published in the United States of America
in 1991 by the Mallard Press.

ISBN 0 -7924-5526-6

Mallard Press and its accompanying design and logo are
trademarks of BDD Promotional Book Company, Inc.

Produced by Mandarin Offset.
Printed and bound in Hong Kong.

Edited and designed by Mitchell Beazley International Ltd.
Artists' House, 14-15 Manette Street, London W1V 5LB.

© Mitchell Beazley Publishers 1991
All rights reserved.

Typeset in Garamond ITC by Kerri Hinchon.
Reproduction by Mandarin Offset, Hong Kong.